BOLD KIDS

African Civilizations

**AMAZING AND INTRIGUING FACTS
CHILDREN'S HISTORY BOOK**

No part of this book may be reproduced or used in any way or form or by any means whether electronic or mechanical, this means that you cannot record or photocopy any material ideas or tips that are provided in this book.

Copyright 2022

All images in this book have been reproduced with the knowledge and prior consent of the artists concerned, and no responsibility is accepted by producer, publisher, or printer for any infringement of copyright or otherwise, arising from the contents of this publication.

Learn about the various cultures in Africa. You'll find a range of interesting facts about early African groups, including rainforest Bambuti, Nigerian Nok, North African Berbers, Bantu from South Africa, and Dutch Boers in South Africa.

Some of these groups developed high levels of government and art, and interacted with other cultures. You'll be surprised to learn how quickly African civilizations grew and changed over time.

ANCIENT EGYPT

The influence of Egyptian culture was sometimes welcomed, sometimes resisted. The indigenous cultures were shaped by Egyptian culture and were sometimes resistant to it.

Some of these differences are reflected in the art and architecture of ancient Africa. This is a brief overview of the history of ancient African civilisations and their impact on the continent. We can also learn about the role played by the Egyptians in the life and culture of Africa.

First of all, the Egyptians were the first people to have a dictator. Their social relations were regulated by scribes and priests. The Pharaoh was a god, king, and high priest all rolled into one.

They ruled the country with an iron fist, owned all of the land, and controlled it through religion. But the privileged Egyptians contributed immensely to the development of mathematics and writing.

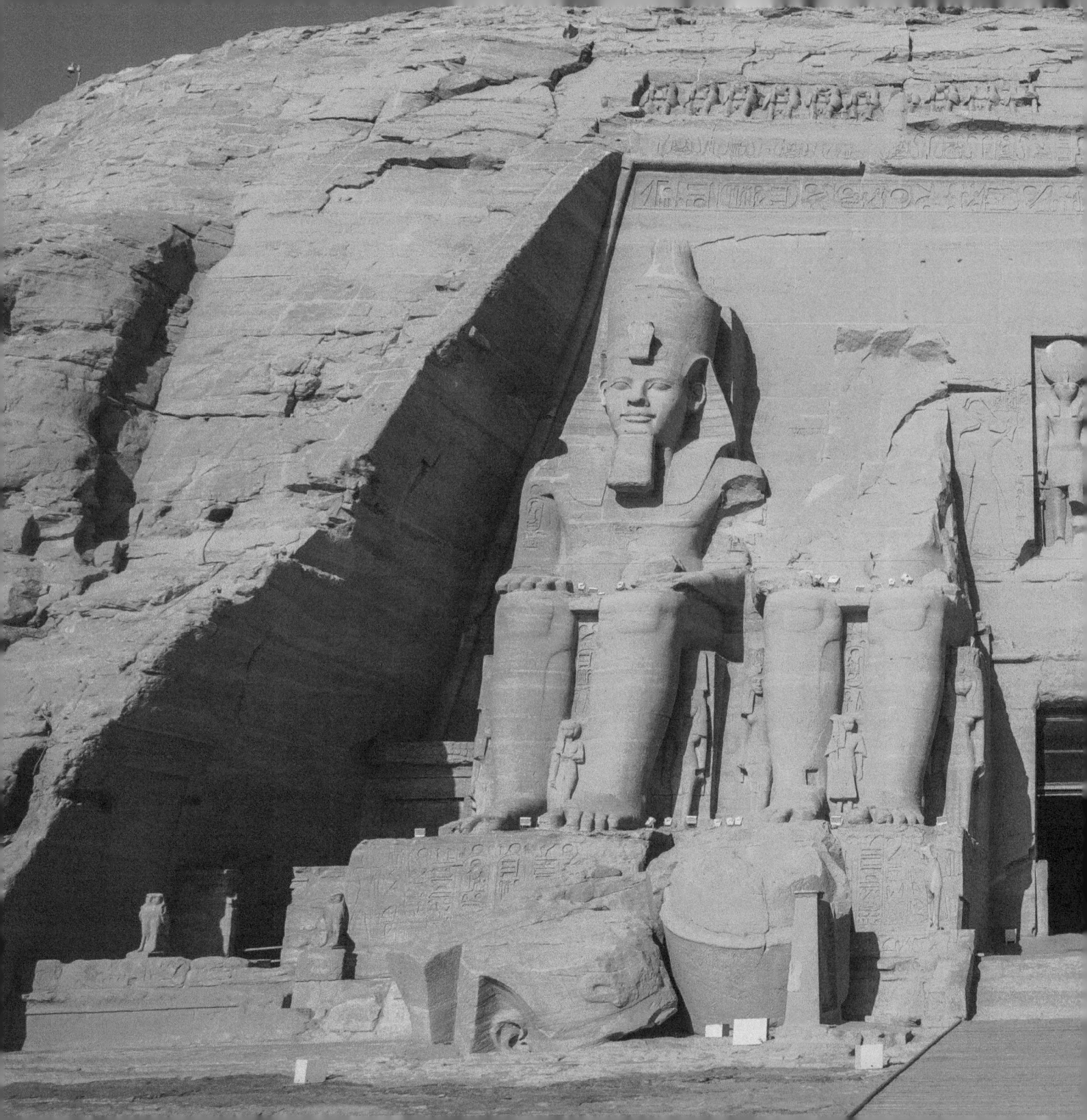

The country was divided into two regions by a long river, the Nile. During this time, the people lived in settlements surrounded by rivers. As a result, they traded goods and traded.

In addition to gold and ivory, they also traded with neighbors from the Far East. They also developed a unique architectural style, including massive stone obelisks. The city was a hub for trade between Europe and Asia.

Nubia is one of the first known kingdoms in Africa. The area was home to rich deposits of gold, and the Egyptians used it for trading. They traded luxury goods through Nubia.

Their kings had archers of exceptional skill and were able to conquer Egypt. This civilization lasted about 100 years. The monuments of their rulers remain today. The region of Nubia was a very fertile region.

TERRACOTTA FIGURES

A team of scientists from the University of Manchester has completed the first biological analysis of ancient terracotta figures found in Ghana. These terracotta figures were carved by an unknown civilization and have become iconic representations of prehistoric African art.

The figures were discovered in Northern Ghana's Koma Land region by Prof. Ben Kankpeyeng. The figures reveal information about clothing, hairstyles, and weapons that can help explain the terracotta figures' sculptural heritage.

The Nok culture of southern Africa produced terra cotta figures in the form of human figures. They were found in a rock-cut cave near the town of Lydenburg.

Based on the similarities between these terracotta figures and the Yoruba art of the early 20th century, these sculptures were created by the Nok culture. However, they may have also served as grave goods and ceremonial offerings.

In Nigeria, terra cotta heads resembled royal figures and attendants. During the Akan period, the high-status Akan nobles commissioned gold regalia, sumptuous textiles, and regal furnishings. These terra cotta heads, carved by female artists, were installed in a sacred grove for a prolonged period.

Though the surface of this magnificent head is eroded by exposure to the elements, its complex hairstyle suggests the creator was a woman of high royal status.

The terra cotta artifacts found at the High Museum of Atlanta underwent a scientific analysis and artistic inspiration. The VMFA's assistant conservator explains how to harvest small pieces of fired clay for TL testing.

He then shares the background of four terra cotta sculptures that she has studied. He also highlights the significance of the Nok terracottas. So, you can learn about the African artifacts that make up this important part of history.

TERRACOTTA WARRIORS

Unlike modern bronze and iron figures, terracotta warriors were cast from moulds, and their heads and facial features are not realistic. Each warrior has his or her own distinctive facial features, but these characteristics are unlikely to be based on a real person's appearance.

However, scholars have determined that there are 10 basic facial shapes common to all terracotta warriors. The warriors are also divided into general categories, including unarmored infantry, standing archers, generals, and lower-ranking officers.

The discovery of the 8,000-strong army of Terracotta warriors was made possible by the work of local farmers who dug up pits near the ancient city of Chang'an, modern-day Xi'an. The figures were placed in the army chamber to accompany the emperor into the afterlife.

The newly discovered terracotta warriors are being restored and conserved. They are part of a huge puzzle that helps unravel the mysteries of the ancient world and the ambitions of the Qin dynasty.

Despite their appearance, the terracotta warriors were constructed with real weapons. They had carefully crafted and carefully preserved weapons. The terracotta warriors were known as mingqi, which is the Chinese word for "spirit articles."

The First Emperor's terracotta army is believed to be portraits of Qin Shi Huang, a 3rd-century state-builder. The terracotta army pieces were discovered in a field near Qin Shi Huang's mausoleum in the early 20th century. The farmer then discovered an underground cave containing a life-sized terracotta warrior.

TRADING

The ancient traders of West and North Africa used gold dust as money. The Akan people mined gold and traded it both locally and internationally.

During this period, traders required a variety of tools and equipment, including boxes to store the dust, scales for weighing gold, spoons for transfer, and brushes to clean the scales. This information provides a valuable insight into the ancient trading culture of the continent. But what was the purpose of this trade? And how was gold dust traded?

As the Mali Empire had been the most powerful state in West Africa, the Songhai Empire followed. This empire prospered by trading sub-Saharan commodities and extracting tribute from its conquered tribes.

In 1471 CE, the Songhai Empire became threatened by a Portuguese fleet sponsored by Lisbon merchant Fernao Gomes. The Portuguese were interested in the lucrative gold fields of southern West Africa and wanted to seize them.

This gold-salt trade was also important in ancient West Africa. The trade between North and West Africa was highly profitable for the people, and the most successful leaders were usually peacemakers.

The seventh century CE saw camel-riding merchants cross the Sahara with gold, and traded it for salt, which was then used as a preservative, flavoring, and a means of keeping moisture in the body. In this way, the trade of gold helped to develop a stable economy throughout Europe.

Milton Keynes UK
Ingram Content Group UK Ltd.
UKHW020619310823
427765UK00009B/92